UN Peace Operations

Part IV

Protection of Civilians

UN Peace Operations

Part IV

Protection of Civilians

Edited by

A K Bardalai and Pradeep Goswami

(Established 1870)

A Joint USI - ICWA Publication

Vij Books India Pvt Ltd
New Delhi (India)

Published by

Vij Books India Pvt Ltd
(Publishers, Distributors & Importers)
2/19, Ansari Road
Delhi – 110 002
Phones: 91-11-43596460, 91-11-47340674
Mob: 98110 94883
e-mail: contact@vijpublishing.com
web : www.vijbooks.in

First Published in India in 2022

ISBN: 978-93-93499-28-8

Contents

Preface

India's deepening engagement with the United Nations (UN) is based on its steadfast commitment to multilateralism and dialogue as the key for achieving shared goals and addressing common challenges faced by the global community. These include those related to peacebuilding and peacekeeping, sustainable development, poverty eradication, environment, climate change, terrorism, disarmament, human rights, health and pandemics, migration, cyber security, space and frontier technologies like Artificial Intelligence, comprehensive reform of the UN, including the reform of the Security Council, among others.

India was among the select members of the UN that signed the Declaration by the UN at Washington on 1 January 1942. India also participated in the historic UN Conference of International Organisation at San Francisco from 25 April to 26 June 1945. India strongly supports the purposes and principles of the UN. It has made significant contributions to implementing the goals of the Charter and the evolution of the UN's specialised programmes and agencies. India believes that the UN and the norms of international relations that it has fostered remain the most efficacious means for tackling today's global challenges. In the spirit of multilateralism, India is steadfast in its efforts to work with the comity of nations to achieve comprehensive and equitable solutions to all problems facing us, including development and poverty eradication, climate change, etc.

India has a long and distinguished history of service in UN peacekeeping, having contributed more personnel than any other country. To date, more than 253,000 Indians have served in 49 of the 71 UN peacekeeping missions established around the world since 1948. Currently, around 5,500 troops and police personnel from India are deployed in eight of 12 UN peacekeeping missions, the fifth-highest amongst troop-contributing countries.

Commencing with its participation in the UN operation in Korea in the 1950s, India's mediatory role in resolving the stalemate over prisoners of war in Korea led to the signing of the armistice ending the Korean War. India chaired the five-member Neutral Nations Repatriation Commission while the Indian Custodian Force supervised the process of interviews and repatriation that followed. The UN entrusted Indian Armed Forces with subsequent peace missions in the Middle East, Cyprus, and the Congo (since 1971, Zaire). India also served as chair of the three international commissions for supervision and control for Vietnam, Cambodia, and Laos established by the 1954 Geneva Accords on Indochina.

India has a long tradition of sending women on UN peacekeeping missions. In 2007, India became the first country to deploy an all-women police contingent to a UN peacekeeping mission. Medical care, veterinary support to the domestic animals of the local population, and infrastructure developmental activities are among the many other services Indian peacekeepers provide to the communities in which they serve on behalf of the organisation.

India has provided several senior mission leaders, including Head of the Mission, Force Commanders, Deputy Head of the Mission, Deputy Force Commanders, and senior staff officers to various missions. Besides the Force Commanders, India also had the honour of providing two Military Advisors, one woman Police Adviser and one Deputy Military Advisor to the Secretary-General of the UN. The first Indian all-women police contingent in a peacekeeping mission, a Formed Police Unit, was deployed in UN Mission in Liberia (UNMIL) in 2007. India was the first country to contribute to the Trust Fund on Sexual Exploitation and Abuse, which was set up in 2016. India's longstanding service has not come without cost; hundreds of Indian peacekeepers have paid the ultimate price while serving with the UN. India has lost more peacekeepers than any other member state.

In the more than seven decades of UN peacekeeping operations and interventions in different kinds of conflict, peacekeepers always faced multiple challenges when it came to implementing the mandate. With the passage of time, these challenges have become more complex, undermining the ability of the peace operations to deliver in the conflict zone. This is also what the Department of UN Peace Operation's survey of August 2019 indicates. Besides the inherent lag between the intent and the outcome in all spheres of the activities, there could be several other strategic and operational reasons for the slow progress of reforms in the field. This is not to conclude that so far, no reform has taken place. Thus India being one of the oldest contributors in peacekeeping operations and, hence, is a vast repository of the best practices.

The United Service Institution (USI) of India in the past has taken the lead in providing the platform for organising discourse and research in the field of UN peace operations to put across an Indian perspective on a few of the most crucial attributes of the current challenges that face reforms of the UN peace operations. At this juncture, USI of India (https://usiofindia.org), the oldest think tank in India, in collaboration with Indian Council of World Affairs (ICWA) (https://www.icwa.in), the premium think tank of India's Ministry of External Affairs, Government of India, planned to conduct a series of webinars on UN peace operations in 2021 on the following themes:

- Theme 1 – India and UN Peace Operations: Principles of UN Peacekeeping and Mandate.
- Theme 2 – UN Peace Operations: Hostage-taking of Peacekeepers.
- Theme 3 – Effectiveness of UN Peace Operations: Dynamics of Composition of Troops and Diversity on UN Peace Operations.
- Theme 4 – UN Peace Operations: Protection of Civilians.
- Theme 5 – Women, Peace and Security.
- Theme 6 – Interoperability Challenges in multidimensional Peace Operations: Role of Senior Mission Leaders (Head of the Mission and Force Commanders).

Inaugural UN webinar was conducted on 27 Feb 2021 on 'India and UN Peace Operations: Principles of UN Peacekeeping and Mandate'. A good comprehension of the meaning of the principles of peacekeeping is important because the way these are interpreted will continue to impact the performance of peace operations. Accordingly, the first webinar was held on the following sub-themes:

- Principles of UN Peacekeeping, its continued relevance and mandate implementation.
- Relevance of the principle of 'Use of Force' in United Nations Stabilisation Mission in Congo (MONUSCO) and United Nations Mission in South Sudan (UNMISS).

- Contribution of traditional peace operations [United Nations Interim Force in Lebanon (UNIFIL) and United Nations Disengagement Force (UNDOF)] for sustainable peace.

The second UN webinar was conducted on 29 Jun 2021 on 'UN Peace Operations: Hostage-taking of Peacekeepers'. Peacekeepers are supposed to be the enablers and get deployed in the conflict zone to help bring peace and save human lives. But when the peacekeepers themselves become the victims, it impacts the effectiveness of the mission. Response to a hostage crisis will depend on several variables which will have to be considered in the hostage rescue strategy. This webinar discussed two different situations necessitating two different approaches with the following sub-themes:

- Overview of the hostage crisis, its implications and tenets of rescue strategy.
- Emerging trends in hostage-taking of peacekeepers.
- Strategy & challenges of hostage rescue when peacekeepers from larger TCCs are taken hostage {United Nations Mission in Sierra Leone (UNAMASIL)}.
- Strategy & challenges when peacekeepers from smaller TCCs are taken hostage {United Nations Disengagement Observer Force (UNDOF)}.

The third UN webinar was conducted on 25 Aug 2021 on 'Effectiveness of UN Peace Operations: Dynamics of Composition of Troops and Diversity on UN Peace Operations'. Diversity matters and affects peacekeeping effectiveness. Mission diversity and effectiveness are falsely assumed to be dichotomous. On the contrary, we can enhance effectiveness by increasing diversity. When Blue Helmets deploy in peacekeeping missions, they carry with them their operational ethos, the way they are trained and cultures and traditions that are unique to different Troop Contributing Countries (TCCs). These characteristics shape the peacekeepers' approach to peacekeeping. This reality presents peace operations with a significant challenge to mandate implementation. In this webinar, the discussion focused on the following sub-themes:

- Effect of composition of troops and diversity – Views of an academician.
- Effect of composition of troops and diversity - Perspective of a practitioner.
- Effects of cultural, social, and military ethos - Perspective of an Indian contingent commander.

The Fourth UN webinar was conducted on 22 Oct 2021 on UN Peace Operations: Protection of Civilians. In any conflict, the innocent civilians are the ones who suffer the most. But the sufferings and effects of intra-state conflicts are more devastating. Millions of civilians get caught up in the conflicts and become victims of the collateral damage. Consequently, Protection of Civilians (PoC) has become the core objective and the primary task of the peacekeeping mandate with the vast majority of peacekeepers getting deployed in protecting the civilians. Peacekeepers, however, are faced with challenges and constraints such as large area of operation and inadequate strength of peacekeepers, adherence to the most controversial principle of peacekeeping – use of minimum force, and rule of law etc. There is also ambiguity in the operational concept of PoC and its applicability on the ground. In the absence of concrete guidance on methods to protect the civilians by the peacekeepers, the mandate implementation becomes more complicated.

Therefore, in this webinar, the discussion is focused on the following sub-themes:

- Protection of Civilians: Concept and the Core Obligation of the UN.
- Protection of Civilians: Challenges of divergent foci of the stakeholders (examples from UNMISS and MONUSCO).
- Protection of Civilians: Perspective from the field.

This monograph is a compilation of talks by eminent speakers during the fourth webinar on 'UN Peace Operations: Protection of Civilians'.

About the Participants

Major General BK Sharma, AVSM, SM (Retd)** is the Director of the United Service Institution (USI) of India. He has tenanted prestigious assignments in India, including command of a mountain division on the China border and Senior Faculty Member at the National Defence College, New Delhi. He represented his country at the UN as Military Observer in Central America and has been India's Defence Attaché in Central Asia. He specialises in Strategic Net Assessment methodology, Scenario Building and Strategic Gaming.

Amb Vijay Thakur Singh is the Director-General, Indian Council of World Affairs. She is a carrier diplomat and had multilateral experience during her service with the Ministry of External Affairs, GOI. She was High Commissioner of India to Singapore and Ireland and prior to that, Joint Secretary to the President of India and Joint Secretary at the National Security Council Secretariat. She also handled Afghanistan and Pakistan desk in the Ministry of External Affairs and was Counsellor in the Embassy of India in Kabul. She was also a Counsellor in the Permanent Mission of India to the United Nations in New York. She retired in Sept 2020 as Secretary (East), Ministry of External Affairs.

Mr David Haeri is the Director of the Policy, Evaluation and Training Division in the UN Department of Peace Operations (DPO). He has extensive field and UN Headquarters experience related to political affairs, peacekeeping, peacebuilding and inter-agency policy development. Previously, he served as the UN-wide Senior

Planning Coordinator for Syria and was the Director of the US$100m multi-donor Joint Peace Fund for peacebuilding support in Myanmar. His field experience includes extended deployments to Cambodia, Liberia, South Africa, East Timor, Afghanistan, and Myanmar.

Major General PK Goswami, VSM (Retd) is the Deputy Director at the USI and Chief Coordinator of the USI UN Peace Operations Faculty. He represented his country at the UN as an Unarmed Military Observer with United Nations Verification Mission at Angola (UNAVEM) in 1991-92. He was also the Senior Faculty Member at National Defence College, New Delhi. He represented National Defence College, India at the 16th ASEAN Regional Forum for Heads of Defence Universities, Colleges and Institutions in Beijing, China in Nov 2012.

Colonel (Dr) KK Sharma (Retd) is a Visiting Fellow at the USI and an Indian Army veteran. He was a military observer in UNTAC, Cambodia. He was an active member in planning and writing of UN Capstone Doctrine on peacekeeping and manuals for trainers in the Office of High Commissioner of Human Rights, Geneva. He has been associated with the planning cell of peacekeeping operations in Indian Army HQ and was a founding member of the Centre for UN Peacekeeping (CUNPK) under the USI of India. He has a PhD in Management from Zurich, Switzerland, and is presently a Professor and Dean, Global Education Programs in Chitkara University, responsible to mentoring and administering UG courses in academic collaboration with the University of Windsor and Trent University, Canada.

Dr Ali Ahmed is an Indian Army veteran, former academic and UN official. His peacekeeping stints as military observer and political affairs officer were in MONUC, UNMISS, UNMIK and UNISFA. He has a PhD in International

Politics from JNU, India and under Special Regulations from Cambridge University. He taught for two years at the Nelson Mandela Centre for Peace and Conflict Resolution. He was a research fellow at the IDSA and an MEA fellow at the USI of India. He is the author of 'India's Doctrine Puzzle: Limiting War in South Asia'.

Dr Cedric de Coning is a Research Professor with the Norwegian Institute of International Affairs (NUPI), where he also co-convenes the NUPI Centre on UN and Global Governance and coordinates the Effectiveness of Peace Operations Network (EPON). He is also a Senior Advisor for the African Centre for the Constructive Resolution of Disputes (ACCORD). He holds a PhD in Applied Ethics from the Department of Philosophy at the University of Stellenbosch in South Africa. His research covers African and United Nations peace and security issues. He has served in several advisory capacities for the African Union and United Nations, including on the UN Secretary General's Advisory Board for the Peacebuilding Fund and co-edited several books.

Brigadier Dhananjay Joshi is a serving Indian Army officer. He commanded a Company as part of the UN Peacekeeping Force in Lebanon, a Battalion in Counter Insurgency operations in the Northeast and a Brigade in high altitude areas in India. Apart from attending the Staff Course at Wellington and Higher Command Course at Mhow, in India, he is a graduate of the US National Defence University, Washington DC. Presently he is posted as a Sector Commander of a composite sector, with troops from Rwanda, Ethiopia and Nepal, in UN Mission in South Sudan (UNMISS).

Major General SB Asthana, SM, VSM (Retd) is presently the Chief Instructor at the USI. He is a former Additional

Director General Infantry of the Indian Army and was CLO in UNMEE. Currently, he is on the Governing/Security Council CEE, IOED, IPC, and other UN Organisations. He is on the Advisory Board of SWEDINT, a member of EPON and the expert group of Challenges Forum. He is a regular speaker at CUNPK and various UN Organisations and IOED representative in UN Headquarters, Vienna, Austria. He regularly participates in media discussions.

Concept Note

UN Peace Operations: Protection of Civilians

Over the past few decades, inter-state conflicts waned but there has been an increase in intra-state conflicts. In any conflict, the innocent civilians are the ones who suffer the most. But the sufferings and effects of intra-state conflicts are more devastating. Millions of civilians get caught up in the conflicts and become victims of the collateral damage.

Violence could be the result of various reasons, including that of social and economic grievances. In intra-state conflicts, the displaced civilians are often targeted. In 1999, the UN Security Council, by adding protection of civilians (PoC) in armed conflict to its agenda, formally recognized PoC as a matter of peace and security.[1] Thereafter, the subject of PoC has found importance in international peace and security.

The HIPPO report found that PoC is a core obligation of the UN as a whole and not only the peacekeepers.[2] But in his report to the General Assembly, the Secretary-General of the UN mentioned that "Empirical research consistently

---

1 UN Security Council Resolution, *The Protection of Civilians in Armed Conflicts,* S/RES/1265 (1999) 17 September 1999

2 UN General Assembly Security Council, *High Level Independent Panel Report,* A/70/95–S/2015/446 (June 17, 2015).

demonstrates that where there are UN peacekeepers, conflict is constrained and there is less violence against civilians".[3]

Consequently, PoC has become the core objective and the primary task of the peacekeeping mandate with the vast majority of peacekeepers getting deployed in protecting the civilians. Peacekeepers, however, are faced with challenges and constraints such as large area of operation and inadequate strength of peacekeepers, adherence to the most controversial principle of peacekeeping – use of minimum force, and rule of law etc.

While there are several tools available to the peacekeepers for PoC, these are at the conceptual level and there are challenges in transmitting the concept of PoC into strategies and practices for their implementation in the field.[4] In the absence of a suitable mechanism, planning and conduct of PoC in the conflict zone becomes complicated because of the varying operating principles of the humanitarian actors and peacekeepers.

Besides, since there is no common 'defined problem' and there are divergent foci of the stakeholders, the relationship between different stakeholders is only that of coexistence rather than that of a meaningful relationship.

Despite the available literature on the subject, several reports and discussions recommending how best to protect the civilians, these challenges are a hindrance to the peacekeepers trying to save the innocent civilians from the scourge of vicious conflicts.

---

3 UN Security Council Report, *The Protection of Civilians in Armed Conflicts*, S/2021/423, May 21, 2021

4 UN, https://peacekeeping.un.org/en/protecting-civilians

In this webinar, the following themes will be discussed:

- **Theme I.** Protection of Civilians: Concept and the Core Obligation of the UN.
- **Theme II.** Protection of Civilians: Challenges of Divergent Foci of the Stakeholders (examples from UNMISS and MONUSCO).
- **Theme III.** Protection of Civilians: Perspective from the Field.

Introductory Remarks

Major General PK Goswami, VSM (Retd)

On behalf of Maj Gen BK Sharma, Director, USI and Amb Vijay Thakur Singh, Director General, ICWA, I welcome all participants to today's webinar.

I am glad to inform you that this year the USI, in collaboration with ICWA, is conducting a series of webinars on UN-related issues. Inaugural webinar, held on 27 Feb 2021 on **'Principles of UN Peace Keeping and Mandate'**, was followed by **'The Impact of Climate Change on UN Peacekeeping Operations'** on 20 Apr 2021 in collaboration with NUPI & SIPRI; **'UN Peace Operations: Hostage-taking of UN Peacekeepers'** on 29 June 21 and **'Effectiveness of UN Peace Operations'** with focus on **'Dynamics of Composition of Troops and Diversity on UN Peace Operations'** on 25 Aug 2021. Today we will deliberate on **'UN Peace Operations'** with a focus on **'Protection of Civilians'.**

After each webinar, all talks are compiled and published as a monograph to share the rich experiences of the panellists with a larger audience for cross-fertilisation of ideas. I am happy to inform you that the Monograph on **'Effectiveness of UN Peace Operations: Dynamics of Composition of Troops and Diversity on UN Peace Operations'** has just been published.

I express my deep gratitude to Col (Dr) KK Sharma, Dr Ali Ahmed, Dr Cedric De Coning from NUPI, Norway and

Brig Dhananjay Joshi from UNMISS, Sudan for accepting USI's request to share their rich experience and deep insight on the **Protection of Civilians in UN Peace Operations**. We are also fortunate to have the presence of a galaxy of UN professionals and practitioners in the event today. My special thanks to Mr David Haeri, Director, Policy, Evaluation and Training Division, UN Department of Peace Operations (DPO) to accept our invitation to deliver the Keynote Address today. Before we proceed further, a few words about today's theme – PoC.

India has always followed the path of 'Dharma' or 'righteous conduct' and it was prevalent in India long before modern humanitarian jurisprudence evolved. The Dharma-based norms for armed conflict in India were founded on the principle of humanity and humanitarian grounds, with high importance attached to distinguishing combatants and non-combatants during armed conflicts. Civilians were not attacked and on the contrary, they had to be protected.

Thus, the need to spare civilians in armed conflict has been acknowledged for millennia, and its origins can be found in early religious texts. However, it is only in the second half of the 20th century that the PoC was firmly universalised and codified following the landmark Fourth Geneva Convention 1949 relating to the PoC in time of war. The need for PoC is now widely acknowledged and has since developed in law, but not much in practice. Thus, now most UN peacekeeping operations have been given PoC as one of the mandated tasks. Accordingly, the need to enhance the operational capability to accomplish the mandate has expanded. But how do UN peacekeepers protect civilians? This is what we will be deliberating today.

Mr David Haeri, Director, Policy, Evaluation and Training Division, UN Department of Peace Operations

(DPO), is a well-known UN professional with extensive field and UN Headquarters experience related to political affairs, peacekeeping, peacebuilding, and inter-agency policy development. Previously, he served as the UN-wide Senior Planning Coordinator for Syria and was the Director of the US $100m multi-donor Joint Peace Fund for peacebuilding support in Myanmar. His field experience includes extended deployments to Cambodia, Liberia, South Africa, East Timor, Afghanistan, and Myanmar. We are indeed fortunate to have Mr David Haeri with us today, and he will deliver the Keynote Address.

Our moderator for the event today is Colonel (Dr) KK Sharma (Retd) who is a Visiting Fellow at the USI and an Indian Army veteran. He was a military observer in UNTAC, Cambodia and an active member in planning and writing of UN Capstone Doctrine on peacekeeping and manuals for trainers in the Office of High Commissioner of Human Rights, Geneva. He has been associated with the planning section of peacekeeping operations in Indian Army HQ and was a founding member of the Centre for UN Peacekeeping under the USI of India. He holds a PhD in Management from Zurich, Switzerland, and is presently a Professor and Dean, Global Education Programs in Chitkara University, Chandigarh, India, responsible for mentoring and administering UG courses in academic collaboration with the University of Windsor and Trent University, Canada.

Keynote Address

UN Peace Operations: Protection of Civilians

Mr David Haeri

Ladies and gentlemen,

I very much appreciate the invitation and opportunity to speak today about the Protection of Civilians (PoC) in UN Peace Operations. Thanks to the United Service Institution of India and the Indian Council of World Affairs for co-hosting this series of events on UN peacekeeping, and especially today's event.

PoC is at the heart of UN peacekeeping in all of our largest missions. It is our greatest ambition, our most critical success, or potentially, the source of our most critical failures. It is also one of our most challenging tasks, and every day we strive to do better and be more effective at protecting tens of millions of civilians across vast areas and with limited resources.

Over the past year and a half, the COVID-19 pandemic has amplified existing protection concerns in peacekeeping settings. However, we are proud to report that – with the support of peacekeeping stakeholders, especially troop and police-contributing countries, such as India – our operations have navigated these tough times and continued to deliver on their mandates, including the protection of civilians. As we begin to see some hope on the horizon of this pandemic, this is an opportune time to reflect on the protection of civilians in UN peacekeeping, the challenges we face, and our future direction.

And what better host institutions for this reflection? India has been a pioneer and a leader in UN peacekeeping, deploying more than a quarter of a million troops in dozens of missions over several decades. Today, this deep dedication is reflected in India's deployment of over 5,000 personnel across nine peacekeeping missions. The three missions with the most Indian deployed personnel – the UN missions in South Sudan (UNMISS), the Democratic Republic of the Congo (MONUSCO), and Lebanon (UNIFIL) – are all implementing PoC mandates in different and challenging circumstances.

India has also been a pioneer towards uniformed gender parity in peacekeeping. India's deployment of the first all-women contingent in a peacekeeping mission, a Formed Police Unit deployed in 2007 to the UN Mission in Liberia (UNMIL), set an example of gender parity in UN peacekeeping. This is an essential part of our outreach to local communities and of our ability to engage with women as well as an important aspect of providing for the protection of civilians and engagement of UN peacekeepers on the ground.

India's support and contributions are a sound investment. According to many studies independent of the UN, peacekeeping remains the most successful multilateral tool available to the international community. However, that doesn't mean we succeed every time – we cope with the most difficult challenges. Despite the increasing number and changing nature of the threats we face, complex environments, dwindling resources, and sometimes absent or stalled political processes, many empirical studies show, unambiguously, that the presence of peacekeepers correlates with fewer deaths, less spread of violence across borders, shorter conflicts, and increased negotiated settlements in civil wars.

I'd like to speak to you today about what PoC in UN peacekeeping is, what challenges we face, and what we need to do better.

PoC in UN Peacekeeping

The protection of civilians from threats of physical violence is currently a priority mandate for six out of 12 peacekeeping operations. Sadly, this reflects the reality that civilians continue to account for the vast majority of casualties in situations of armed conflict, either through direct or indiscriminate attacks. The deployment of a peacekeeping mission often creates an **expectation** that all those at risk will be protected by the mission. But it must be recognized that peacekeeping operations have limited resources and cannot protect everyone, everywhere, at all times. And just as importantly, we must always remember – and remind our host governments – that national authorities have the primary responsibility to ensure the protection of civilians in their territory.

The Security Council has given clear direction that where mandated, **PoC must be prioritised** in decisions regarding the allocation and use of available mission capacities and resources. As a result, strategic decisions must be made by mission leadership about which threats to prioritise – normally those which have the greatest impact on the civilian population or greatest destabilising effect. Missions have developed tools to facilitate this decision making, such as the use of hotspot x-mapping to monitor areas of greatest concern, and then deploy resources accordingly.

We can and should expect that peacekeepers will proactively protect civilians where they can do so. But there is a misconception that equates PoC with direct physical protection by mission uniformed components. PoC is a more holistic approach involving a range of tools across several tiers. The operational concept for the protection of civilians in UN peacekeeping is composed of three mutually reinforcing tiers of action:

(i) protection through dialogue and engagement,

(ii) providing physical protection and

(iii) creating a protective environment. All mission personnel – civilian, police and military – have a role to play across all three tiers.

To be successful, our operations must increasingly focus on **preventing violence** against civilians before it occurs. Our PoC efforts must also be rooted in **community engagement** – responsive to the threats faced by affected populations as well as recognising and supporting the role of communities in their protection. In complex contexts and with limited resources, the **sustainable protection** of civilians can only be achieved through long term solutions that facilitate political conflict resolution, engage communities and support the host state to have the will and capacity to protect its population.

Peacekeeping operations are having an increasing impact through **integrated and tailored protection strategies** that use all of the tools available to the mission and rely on the skills and comparative advantages of civilian, police and military components. In the DRC, MONUSCO has developed comprehensive regional strategies to address the diverse threats in various areas of the country. These strategies, which balance dialogue and political engagement, DDR programmes, and community engagement with the threat of military action, have been successful in reducing threats to civilians. In Mali, MINUSMA has conducted campaigns for the protection of civilians in the northern and central regions, providing a security umbrella for civilian efforts to bring communities together and strengthen local conflict resolution mechanisms, while also supporting state judges to return to these areas and enhance the rule of law. In this context, we have seen the presence of the mission capitalising its skills and resources to then catalyze communities and host institutions, to enhance protection.

Challenges

Despite our best efforts in UN peacekeeping to protect civilians, challenges remain. Peacekeeping operations are increasingly deployed in countries where peace agreements are weak or non-existent, and large-scale violence between armed actors is ongoing. Protecting civilians is paramount in these situations, as civilians bear the brunt of continued conflict. However, ongoing conflict makes our operations risky and difficult and means we often lack genuine protection partners. It can also limit our protection activities: we must focus more on providing immediate physical protection and are less able to engage in establishing a truly protective environment.

This is why it is critical that the protection of civilians be carried out at both the operational and the political levels. We need peaceful solutions to the conflict to create protective environments where civilians are safe. Peacekeeping missions use their good offices and other capacities to resolve conflicts at national and local levels, and thereby avert or at least reduce violence against civilians. For this, the political and protection strategies of peacekeeping operations must be aligned. And they must also be supported and reinforced by the member states and especially the Security Council.

Another challenging situation we face is when **host states limit or impede** the ability of peacekeeping operations to execute their mandates. I would like to repeat and state again, unequivocally, that the protection of civilians is the primary responsibility of the host state. A peacekeeper's first course of action is normally to support the state. Peacekeeping aims to facilitate and support the will and capacity of the host state to fulfil its responsibilities.

Unfortunately, peacekeeping missions currently operate in contexts where the host state limits or impedes the ability of missions to carry out their functions, including for the protection of civilians. For example, in South Sudan and increasingly in the Central African Republic, restrictions are placed on the freedom of movement of the mission. In such cases – which amount to violations of the Status of Forces Agreement (SOFA) between the UN and the host state – active, regular and consistent dialogue with host state authorities is necessary to resolve the issues. While the bulk of this falls to the mission, which must engage on a daily basis on the ground, it is nonetheless a collective responsibility of the Security Council, member states and the Secretariat to ensure that the host state understands its responsibilities and allows the mission to do its work as mandated by the Security Council.

In some even more complex cases, elements of the host state may themselves pose a threat to civilians, for example, security forces engaging in predatory behaviour. The protection of civilians mandate requires the mission to protect civilians regardless of the source of the threat. Our mission will try to engage early and at the highest levels of the host government to prevent such harm as well as to bring such information and advocacy to the attention of the host authorities to address these threats.

But where that engagement is ineffective, as a last resort, the mission may need to interpose itself between civilians at risk and national security forces to protect civilians. Such action is authorised by the Security Council under the PoC mandate, and may ultimately be necessary to save lives.

The final challenge I would like to mention is the need to ensure the sustainability of our efforts, particularly in circumstances of peacekeeping drawdowns and transitions of the UN presence to a different configuration, for instance as we have recently seen in Darfur, Sudan.

All peacekeeping operations are necessarily temporary measures. Therefore, transition planning should start from the inception of a mission and include clear benchmarks for the mission's success and exit. These should be informed by meaningful consultations with host states, civil society and affected communities. Mission protection strategies and protection planning should likewise consider sustainability from the beginning. Tiers one and three of our PoC concept – dialogue and engagement and creating a protective environment – are particularly geared towards longer-term protection. Then, when the Security Council considers reconfiguring, drawing down, or closing peacekeeping operations, it must take into account continuing risks of violence against civilians. Managing such transitions in a way that sustains efforts to protect civilians, in partnership with host states, UN entities and other actors, is critically important. The UN system is working to develop good practices in this area.

Requirements

To face these challenging and evolving contexts, there are several things we need to prioritize.

We need **clear, focused, sequenced, prioritized and achievable mandates** from the Security Council. Now more than ever, member states and the Secretariat need to work together to better tailor mission mandates, configurations and resources to address the needs of conflicts at a specific moment in time.

We also require particular **capabilities** – tailored to each peacekeeping context – to effectively implement the PoC mandate. Peacekeeping operations are increasingly becoming more dynamic and complex and we must ensure to have some of the critical niche capabilities that we need to operate in such challenging environments, such as mobility, situation awareness and peacekeeping intelligence. In most of our areas of operations, we require more units that are agile and offer greater flexibility to missions. Enablers and air assets are vital to ensure that missions facing multiple threats over large areas are nimble and mobile.

We also need more women peacekeepers – civilian, police and military – deployed across all roles and functions. We still have a long way to go to reach gender parity. As discussed previously, more women peacekeepers will enhance our ability to protect all civilians at risk. Additionally, as most peacekeepers are deployed in Francophone environments, French speakers enable us to effectively interact with the local population to understand the threats faced by communities. The upcoming Peacekeeping Ministerial in early December 2021 in Seoul will be an opportunity for member states to demonstrate their commitment to peacekeeping through pledges of these and other critical requirements.

Finally, for the protection of civilians, we need to ensure effective pre-deployment and in-mission **training** on PoC and encourage a **proactive mindset**. To enable an integrated operational approach to PoC, we have developed context-specific PoC training, which has been delivered in the peacekeeping missions in Central African Republic and Abyei (disputed area between South Sudan and Sudan) and will be rolled out in other missions as pandemic travel restrictions are lifted.

In the end, the guidelines, policies and training materials that the Department of Peace Operations puts on paper ensure that all personnel have access to the knowledge that allows them to implement mandates effectively. But we also need personnel who are of the highest calibre and are fully committed to their responsibilities. To protect civilians, we rely on the courage and conviction of peacekeepers in the field, from the leaders of our missions to the civilian and uniformed personnel going on patrol and interacting with communities every day, which is essential to the PoC mandate. We must do everything in our power to protect as many as we can, as this is ultimately the standard by which we will be judged.

Conclusion

In conclusion, it is important to recall that the effectiveness of peacekeeping depends on the commitment and action from all stakeholders – the Security Council, member states, host countries, troop and police-contributing countries, regional partners, the UN Secretariat and the affected communities themselves, that all have to come together to show the effectiveness of our mandates. This need for engagement by all partners is reflected as a key component of the Secretary General's Action for Peacekeeping (A4P) and our current strategy for its implementation, the A4P+. With this initiative, the Secretariat has developed an implementation strategy to accelerate progress and renew momentum on those commitments, including strengthening the protection provided by peacekeeping operations. By focusing on strategic and operational integration, capabilities and mindsets, accountability of peacekeepers, accountability to peacekeepers and other priority areas, including enhancing the transformation of digital technologies in peacekeeping and the implementation of the Women, Peace and Security Agenda across the peacekeeping mandates, we aim to ensure that we can meet the challenges that we are facing.

Thank you again for the opportunity to share these reflections on PoC in UN peacekeeping. I look forward to hearing more about what I'm sure will be a rich discussion today.

Introduction of the Theme

Protection of Civilians: UN Mandate

Colonel (Dr) KK Sharma (Retd)

As per a report of the UN High Commissioner for Refugees (UNHCR)[5], on 09 August 2021, gunmen attacked several villages and killed over 50 civilians in Northern Mali. In Ituri and Kivu provinces of the Democratic Republic of Congo, over 1,200 civilians have been killed so far this year[6]. Early in May 2021, ten attacks were recorded against the humanitarian organizations in an NW town in the Central African Republic (CAR), in which 27 people were killed[7]; and two weeks back, on 06 October 2021, an attack near Bambari of Central African Republic left 15 dead. One of the common factors in all these three countries is, that these have ongoing UN missions with the protection of civilians, as one of their primary mandates. A valid question asked by many concerned groups, therefore, is - Eventually for whose benefit are these Peace Operations established?

---

5 https://www.unhcr.org/news/briefing/2019/8/5d4d2ca94/amidst-escalating-violence-mali-unhcr-issues-new-protection-guidelines.html

6 https://www.africanews.com/2021/09/10/over-1-200-civilians-killed-in-two-dr-congo-provinces-this-year-un//

7 https://reliefweb.int/report/central-african-republic/spike-attacks-against-humanitarian-organisations-nd-l-town

UNHCR 2020 report gives over 82 million displaced people worldwide by the end of 2020[8]. This includes 26 million counted as refugees. This is a result of various conflicts, and most are the victims of collateral damage. During the conflicts of the past 30 years in Afghanistan, Iraq, Myanmar, Syria, Yemen, and a host of African nations, it was the civilian population, which bore the brunt. Consequently, in 1999, the UN Security Council, added protection of civilians (PoC) in armed conflict to its agenda, thus formally recognizing PoC as a matter of peace and security. HIPPO Report[9] in 2015, had listed out top two priorities for the UN - Political Settlement and Protection of Civilians.

Many observers agree that PoC requires a comprehensive, integrated and well-planned, approach to address the challenges that the missions with this mandate face. This was also the foundation of the 2019 protection of civilians Policy[10], which provided a conceptual framework, guiding principles and key considerations for the implementation of the policy. But for the 'formed military units', challenges lie in translating vague concepts of 'protection of civilians' into realistic strategies and operational practices for their implementation. Thus, the issue is more complex than what we tend to believe. Most often, the configuration of the military component as well as humanitarian teams is not commensurate to the PoC tasks, which involves the presence of the UN elements at all vulnerable areas. External spoilers, renegade elements and security contractors complicate the situation further and therefore, the PoC has come under severe criticism from all TCCs and PCCs.

---

8 https://www.unhcr.org/flagship-reports/globaltrends/

9 A/70/357–S/2015/682 dated 2 September 2015 (The future of United Nations peace operations: implementation of the recommendations of the High level Independent Panel on Peace Operations)

10 https://peacekeeping.un.org/sites/default/files/PoC_policy_2019_.pdf

Protection of Civilians: Concept and the Core Obligation of the UN

Dr Ali Ahmed

The obligation of protection of civilians has been implicit in post-Cold War UN peacekeeping mandates. The Cold War stability withdrew from many regions at its end, leading to a rash of conflicts. The post-Cold War consensus in the Security Council allowed the body to innovate with its instrument already available since the Cold War days – traditional peacekeeping. Traditional peacekeeping expanded into wider peacekeeping over the succeeding decade, being applied in many settings in what later came to be termed as multidimensional mandates. Since civilians were victims of violence in most conflicts then, UN peacekeeping operations had to grapple with how to contain and roll back such violence. Peacekeeping operations met with a considerable setback by the mid-nineties, when they were found wanting in coping with the violence against civilians even in areas of their presence as in Somalia, Bosnia and Rwanda. The early promise of peacekeeping operations for addressing such areas of conflict suffered a momentary setback. The hiatus in the late nineties was put to good use and by the turn of the century, the UN was able to conceptualise PoC and deploy the concept to inform peacekeeping mandates.

The paper discusses PoC by first situating PoC in a theoretical paradigm and thereafter appraising the concept itself as it has evolved over the past two decades since its formal inception in 1999. Finally, it seeks to locate PoC in the UN scheme of addressing conflict. The finding is that PoC is a significant aspect of the UN's activity in delivering international peace and security, the organisation's primary purpose. To the extent States remain the foremost actors on the international stage, PoC remains the core obligation of States, with the UN in a supportive role. PoC by the UN can come to the fore temporally and locally in case the state is unable or unwilling to fulfil its obligation as a first-order responder on PoC or itself poses the PoC threat to its people.

Theoretical Prelude

The UN's peace approaches borrow from peace studies theory. A useful start point is the famous conflict triangle in which the three angles (A, B, C) of a triangle are depicted as representing Attitude, Behaviour and Contradiction respectively. Contradiction is the issue in dispute; Behavior is the incidence of violence in the dispute occasions, and Attitudes of distrust are formed by the onset of violence. The model depicts conflict as originating in a dispute, with the ensuing violence giving rise to hostility. Consequently, the threat is not only direct – from violence – but indirect – from the structures (structural violence) and resulting culture (cultural violence). Containing direct violence brings about 'negative peace', but does not go far enough in addressing the root causes of violence, which alone can bring about 'positive peace'.

The UN's approach to peace is cognizant of the conflict model. The UN 'agenda for peace' involves peacekeeping addressing direct violence and bringing about negative peace. Alongside, it addresses root causes for ushering in positive peace by setting back cultural violence in terms of hostile attitudes through peacebuilding, including reconciliation initiatives, and the structural violence that gave rise to the Contradiction in the first place through peacemaking. Thus, it is evident that preserving civilians from violence is not merely protecting them from physical or direct violence but ensuring that the impetus to violence in terms of persisting problem areas and the divides these generate are removed holistically.

PoC Concept

Risks and threats to civilians and the materialization of threats in horrendous violence against civilians has been a facet of conflict through the ages. However, it has gained prominence over the past three decades in intra-state armed conflict. Threats to civilians are in both the short and long term and include political, security and economic factors. Consequently, the UNSC took on board the PoC as a significant part of its mandate to further international peace and security. Starting from 1999, it has actively engaged with the PoC concept, making it over the subsequent 20 years amount to one of the core issues on the UNSC agenda. The UNSC has passed resolutions and presidential statements on PoC, that are not only country-specific, related to peace operations, but also on PoC in general and on PoC themes as sexual violence and children in armed conflict. The UN Secretary-General has also been furnishing the UNSC with periodic reports at its request since the first report in September 1999. These have initially been on an 18-month basis and lately have been annual. The UNSC has convened in open sessions to discuss PoC biannually and in open *Arria* formula sessions on related themes. There is an informal expert group on PoC that informs UNSC deliberations on PoC relevant resolutions. The UNGA Special Committee on Peace and Security also maintains its support for PoC. The UN's latest reform initiative, the Action for Peacekeeping (A4P) includes Protection as one of eight thrust areas. Peace operations have reflected the growing centrality of PoC with the Secretariat developing an operational concept; a Policy, a Handbook, a framework and its PoC-mandated missions have developed mission-wide integrated strategies.

The UN family comprises agencies, funds and programs specifically mandated for programmatic delivery on niche aspects of protection. They concentrate on a rights-based protection approach, including observance of international humanitarian and human rights law, humanitarian access and attending to displaced populations. For its part, a multidimensional peace operation is mandated to support peace processes, promotion, and protection of human rights, building the rule of law and security sector and has specialized mandates on child protection and conflict-related sexual violence (CRSV), besides being tasked with facilitating the delivery of humanitarian assistance. These are also some of the areas of programmatic delivery by the wider UN family comprising the UN Country Teams (UNCT) and the humanitarian country teams (HCT). Multidimensional peace operations have the expertise to engage with protection issues, in conjunction with UNCT and HCT. Structurally, integrated peacekeeping operations ensure unity through the triple-hatted deputy to the Secretary General's special representative, thereby making full use of comparative advantages.

The PoC concept as relevant to peace operations is different from the wider concept of 'protection'. Peace operations, therefore, have to have an integrated approach within for the combined effort of all mission components: civilian, police and military, and a cooperative and coordinative approach with other UN actors. While there is no agreed definition of PoC between the actors, there is a shared objective by these actors to protect civilians from risks and threats to their physical integrity, including those arising from armed conflict.

Peace operations with PoC mandates are specifically required to protect civilians under threat of physical violence. The definition adopted by the Secretariat of PoC explicated in its Policy on PoC reads:

> "Without prejudice to the primary responsibility of the host state, integrated and coordinated activities by all civilian and uniformed mission components to prevent, deter or respond to threats of physical violence against civilians within the mission's capabilities and areas of deployment through the use of all necessary means, up to and including deadly force."[11]

The primary responsibility for PoC is of the host state. Missions are authorised under Chapter VII of the UN Charter to use all necessary means, including the use of force, and if necessary, deadly force. This applies within the limits of the capabilities of the mission and is applicable within its areas of deployment since operations have limitations in terms of resources and locations to which they can deploy. Notable alongside is the primacy of political resolutions to conflicts and the use of force is a last resort and in accordance with the mandate and rules of engagement.

Since multidimensional peace operations by definition have multiple capabilities, each has a separate and interdependent role to play. Reverting to the conflict triangle, it can be said that PoC has to be tackled on all three angles of the triangle: Attitude, Behaviour and Contradiction.

---

11 DPO, 'Policy – The protection of civilians in peacekeeping operations', 2019, p. 6

Corresponding to these angles are the three tiers of PoC action:

Tier I: Protection through dialogue and engagement that corresponds to peacemaking;

Tier II: Provision of physical protection corresponding to peacekeeping; and

Tier III: Establishment of a protective environment evocative of peacebuilding.

The all-of-mission activity in the three tiers is mutually reinforcing. Tier I reflect the high-level panel report's phrase, 'the primacy of politics,' and helps fulfil the role of peacekeeping as the pursuit of sustainable political solutions. The security dimension being predominant, the military and police components are at the forefront in Tier II. Tier III activities are generally planned and undertaken jointly with other partners and in coordination with the UNCT in support of host state authorities and may include security sector reform, disarmament, demobilization and reintegration, rule of law support and capacity building and anti-mine action.

The activities are implemented along with four phases:

(i) Prevention: where anticipated long-term threats are latent and need nipping in the bud,

(ii) Pre-emption: where threats are tangible and likely to eventuate in the short term,

(iii) Response: when threats materialize in the short term, and

(iv) Consolidation: where violence has been contained and relapse needs to be avoided. The last phase serves as a revert to the first phase for future threats, thereby completing a cycle.

PoC as a Core Obligation

The host state has the responsibility for PoC, the UN peace operation acts in support to the state, other than where the state is itself at the origin of the PoC threat, in which case the peace operation is empowered by its mandate to judiciously manage the threat. In doing so, it must keep in mind a principle of peacekeeping: consent of the host state. That it can use force in furthering PoC is in keeping with the other principle of peacekeeping that has it that force can only be used in self-defence and defence of the mandate. Since the mandate enjoins the use of force for PoC, employing force for the purpose is justified. The third principle of peacekeeping – impartiality - is maintained by implementing the policy explicated guiding principles that inform such use of force: inter-alia, last resort, proportionate, mindful of consequences, grounded in international law, under effective command and control and alert to the 'do no harm' dictum.

That PoC is a central priority is amply clear, since elevating suffering and saving lives are consequential objectives in themselves. The Secretary-General in his 2017 report to the UNSC on PoC puts across the idea in the following words:

> "Peacekeepers must always fulfil their core obligation to protect when civilian lives are at stake, but protecting civilians requires far more than physical protection by peacekeepers. It is a whole-of-mission endeavour encompassing civilian, military and police functions such as engaging with local communities, mediating disputes, monitoring human rights violations and gathering information to prevent future violence. This must be complemented by robust political engagement at the international level, including by the Council."[12]

12 UNSC, 'Report of the Secretary-General on the protection of civilians in armed conflict', UN document S/2017/414, 2017, p. 17

To the extent it is a core obligation, it is when peacekeepers are in a position to stall atrocities, mindful of the caveats attending the definition and the guiding principles. Under such circumstances, even the principles of peacekeeping are not to preclude action on part of peacekeepers. Proaction on peacekeepers' part ensures the other three candidate principles of peacekeeping: legitimacy, credibility, and local ownership by people. The last is cognizant of the conceptual challenge state centricity of the international order faces from people-centric concepts as human security.

Limits of PoC

Whereas PoC has acquired priority mandate status among the veritable 'Christmas tree' tasking of peace operations, proactivism on PoC is not without brakes. At Tier I, the political process does not always have the momentum and inclusiveness necessary to preclude PoC threats developing as a consequence. Sometimes the UN is not in a driver's seat when deferring to regional organisations on this count and is left facing the consequences. Where peace processes are slovenly, the 'primacy of politics' suffers. Peacemaking taking a backseat thus increases the premium on Tier II.

At Tier II, there is an impetus to robust peacekeeping that is not wholeheartedly shared by troop and police-contributing countries. There is a continuing subscription to traditional peacekeeping thinking on the use of force. The impetus to robust peacekeeping is also viewed as a spillover from the peace enforcement operations elsewhere in the global war on terror (GWOT), which are incongruent in peacekeeping settings. Whereas the UN peacekeepers do not participate in or conduct anti-terror operations, there are other forces so authorized. This could lead to blue helmets being targeted by armed groups designated as terrorist groups and implicated as adversaries by proximity with forces engaging in peace enforcement and counter-terrorism. This leads to a militarization of peacekeeping, with earlier taboo terms as 'intelligence' now being normalised even in a peacekeeping setting.

Further, the political economy of conflict advantages certain forces, states and their strategic partners. The direction of a political process thereby generates its winners and losers. If Tier I peacemaking concerns position the UN against a 'spoiler' on the ground, who then has to be tempered at Tier II by robust peacekeeping, buttressed by counter-insurgency doctrinal imports from the GWOT arena, this potentially places UN forces at odds with armed groups backed by oppositional political forces. If identity issues lie at the root of such conflicts, then no amount of ministration at Tier III through reconciliation can compensate. All three UN peacekeeping principles are imposed on – impartiality, consent and non-use of force - when tactical level consent is given short shrift in robust operations and separately mandated selective peace enforcement by partner forces. Resultant tension between Tiers I and II leads to a receding horizon for an exit strategy.

Conclusion

The turn of century ascendance of neoliberalism led to growth in the PoC concept. There has been a pushback since, and the world has become multipolar with Russia reemerging and China being the new superpower. This has ended the unipolar moment and the temporal consensus in the UNSC. Troop contributing countries are also chary of having troops placed in harm's way in case of robust peacekeeping. With robust peacekeeping available as a tool, there is more likelihood of leaning on it, rather than using the political process optimally.

PoC proactivism is liable to be mistaken as an external imposition in a conflict environment. Since most conflicts are in post-colonial settings, with former colonial powers usually also serving as pen holders for missions with PoC mandates, PoC messianism may amount to a colonial holdover. Troop contributors cannot serve as mercenaries in enterprises where UN peacekeeping serves as an instrument for parochial interest. Host states also resent and push back through a cultural relativist lens against western liberal values taken for granted as universal. Such foreseeable road bumps temper the notion of PoC being a core obligation for UN peacekeeping. An all-aboard PoC concept and strategy must therefore make haste slowly, taking onboard divergent foci. The next steps must be in league with wider reformative aspects of the UN such as increased representativeness of the UNSC.

References

- DPO, 'Policy – The protection of civilians in peacekeeping operations, 2019
- DPO, 'The protection of civilians in UN peacekeeping: Handbook', 2020
- DPKO/DFS, 'Framework for Drafting Comprehensive Protection of Civilians (POC) Strategies in UN Peacekeeping Operations', 2011
- OCHA, 'Building a Culture of Protection: 20 Years of the Security Council Engagement on the Protection of Civilians', 2020
- José Ramos-Horta, 'Report of the High-level Independent Panel on Peace Operations on uniting our strengths for peace: politics, partnership and

people', UN document A/70/95, S/2015/446, 2015

- UNSC, 'Statement by the President of the Security Council', UN document S/PRST/2015/23, 2015
- UNSC, 'Report of the Secretary-General on the protection of civilians in armed conflict', UN document S/2017/414, 2017
- Boutros-Ghali, Boutros. *An Agenda for Peace: Preventive Deployment, Peacemaking and Peacekeeping*. New York: United Nations, 1992
- John Karlsrud, 'From Liberal Peacebuilding to Stabilization and Counterterrorism', *International Peacekeeping*, Volume 26, Issue 1, 2019, pp. 1-21
- Johan Galtung, 'Violence, Peace, and Peace Research 'Journal of Peace Research', Vol. 6, No. 3, 1969, pp. 167-191

Protection of Civilians: Challenges of Divergent Foci of the Stakeholders

Dr Cedric de Coning

The Effectiveness of Peace Operations Network (EPON) is a global research consortium of more than 40 institutions, including USI-India, that are collaboratively undertaking research into the effectiveness of specific peace operations. EPON has thus far undertaken studies into the African Union (AU) Mission in Somalia (AMISOM), the United Nations (UN) Organization Stabilization Mission in the Democratic Republic of the Congo (MONUSCO), the UN Multidimensional Integrated Stabilization Mission in the Central African Republic (MINUSCA), the UN Multidimensional Integrated Stabilization Mission in Mali (MINUSMA), the UN-AU Hybrid Operation in Darfur (UNAMID), and the United Nations Mission in South Sudan (UNMISS). More will follow. Some of the cross-cutting trends and observations that have emerged from the first studies that have been published give us some insights into the challenges associated with the Protection of Civilians.

Prevention of Large-scale Violent Conflict

Some of the peace operations studied by EPON so far (including AMISOM, MONUSCO, MINUSCA and MINUSMA) have made significant contributions to preventing major civil war and large-scale conflict. The level of violent conflict in these countries would have been significantly worse if these peace operations were not present. Their actions are thus widely understood to have had a deterrent effect and their presence has contributed to preventing large-scale violent conflict. It thus follows that the withdrawal of these operations is likely to result in an increase in violence. Local communities in, for example, eastern DRC or central Mali experiencing violence, or the risk of violence, are seeking the protection of the UN because they believe a UN presence will have a deterrent and preventative effect.

Ending Violent Conflict

Five of the EPON studies – on CAR, the DRC, Mali, Somalia, and South Sudan – suggest peacekeepers are not able to bring about an end to violent conflict in the countries where they are deployed, on their own. EPON has chosen to study ongoing peace operations, rather than those already concluded. Other peace operations, such as those in Côte d'Ivoire, Liberia, Sierra Leone, and Timor Leste, to mention a recent few, have withdrawn after successfully implementing their mandates. However, one significant factor that is different in CAR, the DRC, Mali, Somalia, and South Sudan cases, is the absence of a viable political, governance or peace process that can realistically be expected to bring about an end to violent conflict in these countries. Without such a process in place, the peace operations themselves cannot be realistically expected to end the wars in these countries. These missions simply do not have the political leverage and support, requisite mandates, resources and thus capacity to end or even successfully suppress violent conflict at the scale required. Sustainably bringing an end to the violent conflict can only be achieved politically.

Protection of Civilians

The peace operations in CAR, the DRC, Mali, Somalia, and South Sudan have not met (local and international) expectations when it comes to protecting civilians. The operations have protected many civilians directly and indirectly, but they simply do not have the resources and capacity to always protect all civilians. Several non-military actions, such as conflict resolution, good offices and local peace initiatives, have made a notable contribution to preventing violent conflict and reducing risks to civilians in many instances. The work of most of these operations in areas such as child protection (where the role of MONUSCO in the reduction of the use of child soldiers in the DRC is especially noteworthy), human rights and conflict-related sexual violence is commendable.

A Comprehensive Approach to PoC

Physical protection has a role in deterring risk and responding to incidents, but as is clear from these findings, physical protection cannot resolve the conflicts that generate PoC risks on its own. Peace operations need a comprehensive approach to PoC that covers actions across all three tiers (political, physical and enabling) and that mobilise and integrate the capabilities of a wide range of actors across the political, security, development, environment and rule of law spectrum, as well as across the local to global scales. This requires joint analysis, joint planning, coordination and leadership and joint performance analysis and strategic adaptation.

PoC does not end in and of itself. PoC is only dealing with the symptoms of violent conflict. Peace operations thus need to work closely with local, regional and national leaders and societies to find holistic solutions to the drivers that cause and sustain these conflicts.

One dilemma for peace operations with PoC mandates is the more successful these operations in protecting civilians, the less incentive ruling elites have for seeking the political settlements needed to sustainably bring these conflicts to an end.

Many ruling elites in these contexts prefer a no peace/no war outcome because a political settlement will require compromises and power-sharing. There are all kinds of benefits for these elites and those that seek their patronage from the international presence and their funding, and at the same time, they can blame the external actors for not solving the problem.

Stabilization theory pre-supposes a legitimate state faced with an illegitimate insurgency. What if, however, a state is captured by one set of elites linked to one identity group, and those excluded have genuine grievances related to marginalization and exclusion from the political process and economic participation? In that scenario, a peace operation can be seen by some as a partial actor defending one part of society against another and can be perceived as a party to the conflict by the aggrieved party.

The three core principles of UN peacekeeping (consent, impartiality, and minimum use of force) are designed to prevent the UN from falling into this trap. The further UN peacekeeping moves away from these principles, the more ineffective and unsuccessful it is likely to become. Could this partly explain why the UN's stabilization operations have attracted so much criticism of late, and why the Security Council now seem to prefer Special Political Missions (SPMs), even if the same type of operations would have been labelled as peacekeeping in the past?

This raises the question: should UN peacekeeping operations be deployed with a PoC mandate amidst ongoing conflict? The research findings point to UN peacekeeping being most effective when implementing a ceasefire or peace agreement. That is because such agreements generate consent for the operation, a basis for impartiality, and conditions for minimum use of force. Deploying a UN peacekeeping operation with a stabilization or PoC mandate amid ongoing conflict implies consent only with the host state, lack of clarity to whom impartiality should apply (who are the legitimate political actors?), and unrealistic expectations regarding the utility of the use of force. As Alan Doss recently told Jake Sherman, sending UN forces to protect civilians against the failings of their own government is not a sustainable answer.

Having said that, there is also large n-statistical data of quantitative research that finds that statistically, UN peacekeeping operations do help to reduce violence even amid ongoing violent conflict. See, for instance, Hultman, Kathman & Shannon's Peacekeeping in the midst of war.

There may, thus, be situations where UN peacekeeping is the best or only atrocity prevention instrument available. However, when that happens, it is important for those making these decisions to understand what the limitations of UN peacekeeping operations are, and to compensate for it in other ways, including amongst others accompanying political pressure, adjusting the composition of the mission, targeted sanctions, and the parallel deployments of other organizations or forces, such as the African Union, that may be in a better position to use force, if that is what the situation requires.

Ultimately, the best protection is a political settlement that ends violence against civilians. Stabilization operations and Protection of Civilians mandates amidst ongoing conflict tend to result in no peace/no war frozen conflicts with regular massacres and daily sexual and gender-based violence. The EPON findings to date suggest that UN stabilization operations can reduce the violence but can't end it without a political settlement. This is why there has been such a focus on the primacy of politics in peacekeeping. Stabilization and Protection of Civilians should not become the goal. The goal is reaching, implementing and adapting political settlements that produce and sustain peace. Stabilization and Protection of Civilians are important mid-way objectives to reduce suffering, but when it becomes a goal in and of itself we end up with frozen conflicts where the peacekeeping operation itself becomes part of the problem.

UN peacekeeping has shown a remarkable capacity to adapt continuously to new challenges over the past 70 years, and there is no evidence to suggest that it will not continue to do so into the future. As researchers, we should stimulate this adaptive process by focussing attention on those aspects that have proven to be effective, and caution against those that have proven to be ineffective, by continuing to generate evidence of the factors that influence UN peace operation effectiveness via both comparative and longitudinal research studies.

As Mateja Peter and I argue in UN Peace Operations in a Changing Global Order, despite the significant changes currently underway in the global order, and the uncertainties that come with such turbulence, most countries and regional blocs, such as the African Union, European Union, the Nordic region and the BRICS (Brazil, Russia, India, China and South Africa), agree on and repeatedly emphasize the importance of the UN as the centrepiece of global governance and a rules-based multilateral order. Despite changes at the macro-level, the comprehensive reforms of the UN's management, development, and peace and security structures, the significant attention that is rightly being focussed on prevention, and the current preference for SPMs mentioned earlier, UN peacekeeping is likely to remain the flagship enterprise of the UN. This is because UN peacekeeping remains the most visual embodiment and achievement of the post-World War II multilateral system of global governance. Over the past 70-plus years, more than one million troops from more than 110 nations have participated in 70 UN peacekeeping missions. This is a remarkable achievement in collective security and global governance, and the UN and international community are not likely to abandon or radically transform peacekeeping as an institution with such a rich and successful history.

Protection of Civilians: Perspective From the Field

Brigadier Dhananjay Joshi
(Sector Commander: UNMISS)

Introduction

Protection of civilians in the context of United Nations peacekeeping is defined as "all necessary action, up to and including the use of deadly force, aimed at preventing, pre-empting or responding to physical violence or threats of violence against civilians, within UN capabilities and areas of operations and without prejudice to the responsibility of the host government". This definition is distinct from but complementary to the definition used by the humanitarian community which terms protection as "encompassing all activities aimed at obtaining full respect for the rights of the individual in accordance with international humanitarian, human rights and refugee law".

PoC is now integral to the mandate of most UN peace building and stabilisation missions. It aims at creating a secure and stable environment which is a core function of peacekeeping. While the primary and sovereign responsibility to protect civilians inside its border rests with the host country, UN missionsare fully empowered and obliged to act unilaterally, when necessary. For instance, in the case of UN Mission in South Sudan (UNMISS) the Security Council has qualified the mandate to expressly direct that "*The protection of civilians must be given priority in decisions about the use of available capacity and resources within the mission".*

This paper will highlight experiences from the field in UNMISS to outline the challenges faced and strategies adopted to translate the vision of PoC into action. The situation in many other countries would be similar and therefore, the lessons will find resonance.

PoC – the Larger Canvas

PoC should not be seen as just providing security. In the context of operations by the UN, it has five dimensions:

- Preventing violence.
- Physical protection of those escaping from violence.
- Strengthening overall human security.
- Providing security to humanitarian workers.
- Spreading awareness and building respect for human rights.

The **first** one is preventing violence. The consequences of armed clashes can be staggering. Therefore, every effort must be put in to pre-empt and deter violence. This calls for a robust intelligence network and maintenance of a high degree of situational awareness. The aim being to pick up signs of brewing tension, engaging with community leaders and political elites and being proactive. Dialogue and engagement can help build resilient communities who can maturely handle provocations and break the cycle of revenge attacks. UN presence has a sobering impact during tensions and therefore patrolling and maintaining visibility is important and acts as a deterrent againstviolence.

The **second** dimension is physical protection. Violent conflict creates refugees andIDPs. It becomes the duty of UN to protect those who are escaping from violence or imminent threat of violence. Even where people have not directly sought its refuge, it is the duty of the UN to reach out and bring them under a prophylactic security umbrella.

Any large-scale violence leads to displacement which in turn results into loss of livelihood. The Internally Displaced People (IDPs) face hunger, starvation, disease, and death every day. Their camps invariably become huge slums where clean water, sanitation, public health, and medical care are live challenges. Crime and ethnic polarisation of communities within the camp are also realities. Women and girls are especially susceptible to exploitation and abuse. Therefore, sound management of these camps and rendering of humanitarian aid to those affected is essential.

The **third** dimension is strengthening overall Human Security. In poor countries, food scarcity is both a driver and a consequence of conflict. Human Security can prevent conflict and mitigate its effects. Climate change can have a devastating impact on communities pursuing subsistence farming and nomadic pastoralism. Measures to address the cycle of draughts and floods and drawing strategies to offer alternate livelihood to people is important. Many of the countries facing violence and displacement are also the ones witnessing a population explosion. The fragile infrastructure can barely sustain the present population and will get overwhelmed by the added millions. Therefore,rapid yet sustainable development is important.

The **fourth** dimension is providing security to the humanitarian workers. At places torn apart by violence, delivery of food and medical aid is vital. Otherwise far more will die of hunger and disease. But a state of lawlessness makes it extremely dangerous for humanitarians to operate by themselves. Security provided by the UN peacekeeping contingents enables other civilian partners like the WHO, WFP, or UNICEF to operate with confidence. Thus, PoC cannot be achieved unless the aid givers themselves are protected.

The **fifth** dimension is the strengthening the respect for human rights. Sex and Gender Based Violence (SGBV) and Conflict Related Sexual Violence (CRSV) are so rampant at places that they are unfortunately taken as normal. Patrolling by the UN and engagement with communities is essential to spread awareness and encourage people to talk about violations. The monitoring, investigation and reporting of violations puts pressure on the Government to control such acts and bring the perpetrators to justice.

Operational Challenges

The challenges posed by the operational environment during UN PoC mandates stem from the following three factors:

- Accountability and rule of law.
- Nature of conflict.
- Area of operations versus availability of resources.

Accountability and Rule of Law

UN presence in a country is meant to be an enabler. But in the context of PoC, we usually face two scenarios. First, where the Government is *not able* to provide security and second where despite capacity, it is *unwilling* to provide security. The former could be due to weak territorial control, lack of resources or weak institutions. The latter is invariably due to political reasons. Out of the two, the latter situation is more challenging because it often pits UN peacekeepers at cross purposes with the local law enforcement agencies. This creates a dangerous and frustrating operational environment.

Often, there may be a mix of both the scenarios within a country at the same time.

This is typically the case in South Sudan which gained independence in 2011. UNMISS started with a mandate to build state capacity in the newborn nation. Unfortunately, in 2013 within two years of independence, the government and the army split into multiple factions plunging the nation into a civil war. The war left over 400,000 people dead, 1.6 million displaced internally with another 2.2 million refugees in neighbouring countries. In 2018, a Revitalized Peace Agreement came into force. The ceasefire is holding but peace remains fragile.

Presently the country is governed by a Transitional Government. The National Assembly is not fully formed, and the constitution is still in the making. The central ministries and State Governments are headed by military generals of different factions in a power sharing arrangement. The Peace Agreement calls for unification of all the armed groups into the South Sudan People's Defence Forces (SSPDF). But the unification is incomplete. In addition, there are rebel groups who have not signed the Peace Agreement and are still fighting against the transitional Government. The economy is poor, and the country is surviving on foreign aid. The Government is unable to pay salaries and departments get little or no funding. In such a milieu, we find shades of both 'unable to protect' and 'unwilling to protect'. The typical realities for a peacekeeper are:

- ➢ The degree of cooperation from the law enforcement agencies varies from place to place, time to time and context to context. Access denial is a common problem where UN patrols are blocked from visiting sensitive places to investigate violent incidents and human rights abuses.

- Killings and sexual violence are often committed by government soldiers and policemen themselves. Either as stand-alone crimes or as part of revenge attacks against communities accused of helping rival factions. UN peacekeepers must maintain a fine balance where they monitor and report abuse by the very same people with whom they interact every day.

- UN must also be careful not to be seen as an occupation force or a military force acting on its own. At the same time, it cannot afford not to act if the Government forces failed to act.

- UN is accused of taking sides and helping one faction versus the other. It is deliberately done to keep it under pressure. Humanitarian agencies are often targeted to dissuade them from operating in rival territories. Though the organised forces have never attacked the UN, false accusations can instigate attacks by vigilante groups and tribal militias.

Nature of Violence

In South Sudan, the population of 13 million is composed of 64 different tribes. As in many other places, tribal identity is very deep and overshadows a common sense of nationhood. The political factions and armed groups are largely organised along tribal lines. The various generals have their own loyalist units drawn from their own tribes. Apart from the politically organised groups, there are numerous community and tribal militias.

As result of the liberation struggle and civil war the country is flooded with arms. It is common to find even cattle herders armed with AK 47s. The rural economy is pastoral and revolves around cattle. While cattle raids between communities have always been a way of life, the proliferation of lethal weapons has brought a new dimension of brutality to the tradition. Thus, violence can escalate rapidly involving mass killings, burning of villages, looting and severe human rights abuses. The scars of such large-scale violence are not easily forgotten and become the source of a continuing cycle of revenge.

Though there is no fighting between the major political factions at the national level, lethal violence at the local level is common. Local militias are often used as proxies by the bigger political factions to gain influence. Violence is orchestrated to build grounds to sack inconvenient political rivals. Some violence is also attributable to groups who want to be heard and create political space for themselves during the present crucial phase when the constitution is being framed and administrative boundaries are being redrawn.

Irrespective of the fact whether the violence is politically driven or due to local dynamics, the humanitarian impact is the same. From the perspective of UN and PoC the realities are as follows:

- Violence displaces people. Even as the return and rehabilitation of the people displaced during the Civil War is slowly being facilitated, any fresh violence creates new waves of displaced people.
- In fertile tracts, the land of displaced communities has been taken over by others. This makes the task of return, rehabilitation, and reintegration of refugees and IDPs extremely difficult. It can lead to fresh bouts of violence.
- Whenever violence breaks out, the IDPs invariably seek refuge next to UN sites or the international NGOs or the Church. During the Civil War, more than 110,000 people poured into five UN bases in

South Sudan seeking protection. While comprising only 10 percent of the displaced community, the five PoC sites presented new and distinct challenges for the UN.

- Many humanitarian agencies, some acting alone and some under the UN umbrella, are working to provide food and medical aid to communities impacted by violence. But the state of lawlessness makes South Sudan one of the most dangerous places for these humanitarians. Banditry, killing of aid workers and looting of aid is common.

Area of Operations versus Availability of Resources

South Sudan is a big country. It is 900 km East to West and 600 km North to South making it larger in size than France or Germany. Covered with equatorial forests, grasslands and swamps it has just 250 km of metaled roads. Heavy rains and flooding make all dirt tracks impassable for six months in a year. Owing to the soft sticky soil, any cross-country movement of vehicles is impossible. Therefore, surface mobility is practically absent. Mobile phone connectivity and electricity is available only in a few large towns. The rest of the country, especially the countryside, is living in the dark ages. For UN peacekeeping operations, the implications are:

- The country is vast. Distances are huge. It is impossible for the UN to be everywhere. Switching of forces is not possible. Forces once committed in a location will remain there. Therefore, mapping of hotspots and correct siting of the operating bases is extremely important.

- Each base has to be self-contained in terms of manpower, vehicles, specialist equipment, security, communications, medical, administration and logistics.

- The wear and tear of vehicles and equipment plying on non-existent tracks is extremely high. At a human level the high heat, humidity and malaria infested forests also take their toll.
- Sustenance of all the far-flung UN operating bases is mostly by air. Rotation of troops and delivery of supplies is also by air. Thus, the cost of maintaining the mission is extremely high running into over a billion dollars annually. Thus, thereis a constant push to downsize with the improvement of the security situation. But the reduction in force levels and closing down of operating bases has to be a very calibrated decision.

Conduct of Operations

Deployment

In terms of deployment, the system followed in UNMISS is the 'grid' pattern of operating bases with a 'hub and spokes' concept of ops. Each battalion or company operating base acts as the hub while the patrols that it sends out act as the spokes. Thus,the entire area is covered by foot, vehicle, river or aerial patrols. The patrols may be shortor long duration lasting from one to 14 days. At times platoon sized Temporary OperatingBases (TOBs) are established in sensitive areas for up to three months or more.

The UN has graduated from pure peacekeeping missions to 'integrated missions'where the force element is one among many components. In UNMISS the civilian verticalincludes sections for political affairs, gender, human rights, refugees, UN Police etc. Themilitary component comprises the troop contingents and the Military Observers. The humanitarian actors include the WFP, UNICEF, WHO, UNHCR etc. All stay in the same base and work in unison to fulfill the mandate. Thus, most patrols taken out are 'IntegratedPatrols' which are coordinated at the joint civil military set up called the Field Integrated Operations Centre (FIOC). Each patrol that goes out delivers humanitarian aid, engageswith community leaders, interacts with the local security forces, civil administration, women, and NGOs. It picks up signs of brewing tensions and notes grievances for action.

PoC Camps

The PoC sites or camps in South Sudan are a unique consequence of the civil war. Never on such a large scale, have IDP settlements existed within or near UN peacekeeping bases. In the beginning they were protected by armed peacekeepers which witnessed the blurring of civil and military lines. Thus arose the need to incorporate UN Police to take over their management and relieve the military for other tasks. It has been seven years that the PoC sites came into being. It was felt that despite an improvement in the security situation, the IDPs were unwilling to return, and the camps were acquiring a permanence.

Therefore, since end of 2020, the PoC sites are one by one being handed back tothe South Sudanese authorities. They are now called IDP Camps. Humanitarian assistance is still provided but the security and management rests with the Government. As on date four out of the five camps have been handed over and only one remains at Malakal.

Lessons Learnt

Limitation of PoC Efforts. PoC is meant to plug a gap in governance delivery but can never replace the Government. In the absence of governance and widespread lawlessness, peacekeeping efforts do count and do save lives but are unable to bring a substantial change in the near term. PoC is the immediate aim in conflict situations, but it cannot be an end in itself. It must go hand in hand with the political process to address the root cause of the conflict. Reconciliation, inclusive governance, and development should be the ultimate aim.

Women Peacekeepers. Considering that women and girls are most vulnerable to violence, discrimination and exploitation in a disrupted society, the ratio of female peacekeepers is very low. Troop contributing countries are unable to provide adequate women combatants. Male peacekeepers are not suited to interact with local women andso gain only half the perspective. Increasing women participation will yield better situational awareness and better response.

Language Assistants. In a country with scores of languages and dialects, the gaining of local perspective suffers from the availability of translators who are fluent in the local languages as well as English. Often even the locals speak only one or two of the many languages. Therefore, the requirement of different Language Assistants is huge and so far, has not got much attention.

Conclusion

Protection of Civilians is about Human Security as a whole, beyond the immediate demands of physical protection against violence. Security of those hit and displaced by violence cannot be ignored. At the same time the security of humanitarian workers and their programs is vital to reconcile, stabilise and build resilient societies. PoC is therefore a huge task and UN cannot reach everyone. Missions must prioritise their presence and activities by reaching out to the most needy and maximum numbers. UN cannot supplant state institutions even if they are weak or subverted. It has to work with them. Where there are multiple factions with deep distrust,maintaining neutrality is a must. It is not just important for peacekeepers to be impartial and transparent but equally important to be seen as such. When institutions and procedures are weak, rapport and personal equations matter. UN peacekeepers, especially officers must have excellent leadership qualities and interpersonal skills. While the mandate gives the peacekeepers the authority to open fire, the biggest weapon with the UN is the moral force and respect that it carries. The discipline and personal conduct of peacekeepers is extremely important. There is no scope for misdemeanors.

Protection of Civilians in UN Peace Operations: Key Issues

Major General S B Asthana, SM, VSM (Retd)

Backdrop

The issues regarding PoC and use of force are being flagged in context of the seminar held jointly by USI of India and ICWA on the subject on 22 October 2021. Bulks of the peacekeeping missions today are stabilization missions having the role to PoC in built in the mandate. Almost 95 percent peacekeepers are mandated for PoC in some form or the other. The nature and frequency of conflict is changing from inter-state to intra-state with increasing involvement of non-state actors and threat to lives of innocent civilians.

Is it a Core Obligation?

The HIPPO[13] report highlighted that Human Right of people is as important as sovereignty, and the protection of civilians is an unavoidable expectation and obligation of the UN, wherever its peacekeepers are deployed. The peace operations therefore need to adopt a balance between people centric approach besides state centric mandated approach. It supplemented the UN Security Council Resolution on The Protection of Civilians[14] in Armed Conflicts, of September

13 UN General Assembly Security Council, *High-Level Independent Panel Report,* A/70/95–S/2015/446 (June 17, 2015).

14 UN Security Council Resolution, The Protection of Civilians in Armed Conflicts, S/RES/1265 (1999) 17 September 1999

1999, enhancing its scope to cover intra-state conflicts and violence. While UN peace operations are not launched for counter insurgency operations (COIN) or counter terror operations, in reality, the peacekeepers deployed in stabilisation missions get inadvertently sucked in such operations; hence there is a need for being ready for it, whenever situation so demands.

Challenges to PoC

With increased presence of non-state actors in the mission areas involved in violence, it is necessary that the peacekeepers have the requisite capacity to deal with it. The first and foremost is a strong mandate, which is implementable along with the need for adequate force to do so in terms of right composition of military, police and civilian components, adequately trained for the envisaged role thus enhancing the need for pre-deployment training. The requisite troop density is also essential, UNMISS and MONUSCO being cases in point.

Peacekeepers need adequate equipment in terms of military hardware, technological empowerment in terms of capacity and resources, keeping in view the capacity of TCCs, as well as the host state. There is an inescapable need for actionable situational awareness in PoC activities, which also requires digital empowerment and technological upgrade of TCCs. India has recently offered to make situational awareness toolkit for peacekeepers during its recent tenure as President of UNSC.

Use of Force

It is seen that the articles in UN Charter and Resolutions related to use of force are silent on use of force against non - state actors, who are increasingly being seen as threat to civilians as well as peacekeepers. In some cases there is also a need for PoC from state/state sponsored forces. In doing so, the mission leaders and peacekeepers on ground have to act under apprehension of being accused of partiality/ favouritism by the party causing violence. The media and HR activism also adds to the hesitation of commanders on ground. UN needs to have clearer policies for such contingencies. The non-state actors don't follow any mandate/SOFA/ ROE; hence have an advantage over peacekeepers, who are regularly scrutinised for quantum and proportionality of use of force. The Cruz Report and A4P highlight the aspect of protection of peacekeepers in view of increasing casualties of peacekeepers. Currently the mission leaders on ground have to find own innovative methods to deal with PoC as well as fulfilment of mandate.

There is also a need for a necessary legal framework to protect peacekeepers without disturbing the consent of parties. The use of modern surveillance equipment requires deliberations as some host nations may not be comfortable with it. The revision of mandates also has to be faster because it's often seen that the situation on ground changes much faster than the change in mandate.

Summary of the Proceedings

Colonel (Dr) KK Sharma (Retd)

On theme – Concept and the Core Obligation of the UN, Dr Ali Ahmed expressed that the threat to civilians is in short and long term both and includes various factors. Major take away could be the understanding of PoC through tiers giving a theoretical structure to the discussion. The tiered PoC was very well elaborated in that Tier I calls for protection through dialogue and engagement; Tier II desires provision of physical protection; and, finally Tier III is for establishment of a protective environment. Most important take is that any robust peacekeeping is likely to place UN forces at odds with armed groups and political forces in the host country – Mali, Somalia and former Yugoslavia could be apt examples. Robust force application takes peacekeeping to enforcement, which in the long run is considered unviable and undesirable. Dr Ali also explained that the PoC can not be the core concept of PKO, though it may be a major task or concern.

On Challenges of divergent foci of the stakeholders (with excellent examples from UNMISS and MONUSCO), Dr Cedric spoke about then political, physical and enabling environment, as a three tier structure. Host Government, local Communities and Humanitarian elements, all play their part in the PoC. The exposition also brought out a very important role of various humanitarian units in the field. To succeed in the PoC mandate, Dr Cedric emphasised on the coordination among various stakeholders, for which joint strategy – assessment, planning, execution and sharing of information are most important.

Giving his perspective from the field, as a sector commander in an ongoing mission in South Sudan, Brig Dhanjay Joshi very lucidly identified the key challenges in implementing PoC mandate. One of these was that a host country being unable to protect or unwilling to protect, itself is a major challenge to any peace operation. As was often said, there has to be some peace to keep. Brig Joshi also amply brought out that success in PoC directly correlates to the support from the host nation, whose resistance can undermine all UN efforts. As a sector commander, he brought out the challenges of converting PoC sites into IDP and associated challenges of providing security and other logistical arrangements. Very important challenge and suggestion came that in view of the vulnerability of women and girls for violence in a conflict area, the UN needs to increase the ratio of female peacekeepers.

Special Remarks

Major General BK Sharma, AVSM, SM & Bar (Retd)

Thank you Colonel (Dr) KK Sharma (Retd) for those kind words. I think it has been a very fascinating session today, and my special thanks to Amb Vijay Thakur Singh for having very patiently sat through the whole proceedings. My gratitude to Major General PK Goswami, Major General (Dr) AK Bardalai and Mr David Haeri from UN Department of Peace Operations (DPO; for their efforts to make this event a success. Also thanks to the other speakers Dr Cedric de Coning, Dr Ali Ahmed and my colleagues from the Army, Brigadier Dhananjay Joshi.

Today's discussion has reinforced my impressions gathered from UN as a military observer in ONUCA - a mission in Central America that was mandated inter-alia disarming and demobilization of CONTRAS. Honduras was being used by the Americans to support CONTRAS against Sandinista. ONUCA mission comprised UN participation from various countries and the mission included operations in the five Central American Countries. A large number of agencies were involved in the rehabilitation of CONTRAS in Nicaragua. That model of UNPKO we can easily apply to Afghanistan in times to come. What stood out was that the diversity of troops from various countries if optimally cross-pollinated can be a great advantage in making the missions more representative with systematic check and balances.

The USI has good partnership with ICWA with potential to expand it to the Challenger Forum, NUPI and EPON. The USI has rich faculty comprising senior diplomats and force commanders and even were consulted by the High Level Independent Panel on UN Peace Operations (HIPPO) panel on the UN reforms. Mrs Thakur Vijay Singh herself has been at our UN Mission in New York. It is high time that we put our heads together and provide perspective on the UN issues pitched at policy and doctrinal levels. The character and the nature of UN peacekeeping operations have undergone a dramatic change. Modern conflicts are rooted in multi-domains in the grey zone environment characterized with volatility, uncertainty, complexity, ambiguity. There is a need to critically analyse the dynamics of existing and emerging conflict zones and application of technology in the UNPKO. Lessons from Iraq and Syria are the harbingers of the challenges ahead. Peacekeeping is no more enough for durable peace, for that we need a sustainable peace building mandates and capacities. UN related research institutions must carry out a 360 degree diagnostic assessments of some of these conflict zones, look at certain flash points, inflection points, triggers and then formulate proactive strategic response with a mission of responsibility to protect then doing the firefighting. To that extent, I would urge Director CUNPK here to involve ICWA and USI in running certain scenario-based table top exercises which is the core competency. As think tanks our endeavour should be to provide the MEA, MOD, and associated government agencies well-researched inputs for refining the policy-frameworks. I am sanguine that the series of monographs produced after these webinars will serve that purpose aptly. With these words, I thank all participants once again and we look forward to more thematic and intellectually stimulating sessions in the days ahead.

Closing Remarks

Amb Vijay Thakur Singh

Today's discussions have been extremely informative and detailed. I would like to thank Mr. David Haeri for his keynote address, Col Sharma and all panelists for their insightful remarks. ICWA and USI are collaborating on a series of webinars related to UN Peace Keeping Operations and this was the 4th webinar with focus on Protection of Civilians.

UN peacekeeping operations are an essential tool, at the hands of the international community, for maintaining global peace and security. A few decades ago, most UN peacekeeping operations were engaged in post inter-state conflicts, once a ceasefire was agreed. Today, in contrast, more than two-thirds of the UN's peacekeepers are involved in more complex intra-state conflicts. These new circumstances have brought peacekeepers into close contact with civilian populations without any ceasefires agreements in place.

Today's discussion showed how violence as a result of intra-state conflicts between different warring groups has increased the complexities of UN peacekeeping operations. It tests the capability of UN Peace Keeping Operations (UNPKOs) to not only bring back peace in conflict zones but also to deal with the issue of innocent civilians caught in conflicts. This is a challenge for the UN.

Historically, the first resolution on the PoC was adopted by the UN Security Council in 1999. Later, with the "Responsibility to Protect Doctrine" passed by the UN General Assembly in 2005, the international community accepted greater responsibility for protecting civilians from atrocities.

Given the changing nature of emerging security challenges, UN peacekeeping practice on Protection of Civilians has continued to develop, to reflect evolving operational methods and approaches to effectively implement PoC mandate. The 2015 PoC guidelines provide for a three-tiered approach to protect civilians. Tier I — protection through dialogue and engagement; Tier II — provision of physical protection; and Tier III — establishment of a protective environment. The concepts of these guidelines have been generally endorsed by the member states.

Discussions today have reflected on some issues regarding the importance of a multi-dimensional approach to UNPKO and, in this context, the need for integrated approach of all aspects of PoCs. India has long held that both the civilian and military components need to deliver for the Mission to succeed.

Policymakers need to take continuous steps towards closing gaps that exist between situations of the plight of civilians in armed conflicts and the necessary action of bringing appropriate responses. For these issues, we need to look at the following:

- Addressing Critical Gaps. UN currently lacks critical enabling capabilities such as intelligence acquisition, force sustaining capabilities, rapid reaction capabilities, among others. These gaps need to be addressed.

- Training of Peacekeepers. Complex missions require peacekeepers from various backgrounds and experiences to be trained to achieve common standards and capabilities. This is important for Protection of Civilians.

- Technology and Innovation. Technology can be harnessed to assist mission accomplishment. Technology that is proven, cost effective, reliable under field conditions and enables early warning and early response, is required.

- The role of women peacekeepers in the protection of civilians is important.

In conclusion, the UN system as a whole, working closely with member states, should look at these issues to achieve the goal of protection of civilians in conflict situations.